CONTENTS

Copyright © Marvin's Magic ® 2003

3 London Road, Markyate, Herts, AL3 8JL, UK

www.marvinsmagic.com

Published by Alligator Books Ltd, 155 Regents Park Road, London NW1 8BB

Printed in China

THE GROWING ROPE

Effect: A short rope grows into a long rope!

Secret: For this trick you will need a length of soft rope. Before your show, secretly push the middle section of the rope up your sleeve so that all that remains are the two ends. If you hold the rope as shown in the picture it will appear to your audience that you only have a short rope. Begin to pull the ends and slowly the rope will appear to grow before your spectator's eyes!

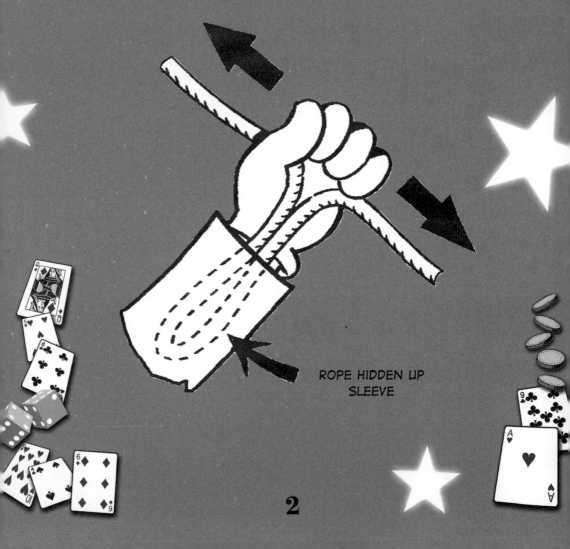

ROPE HIDDEN UP
SLEEVE

NOT A KNOT?

Effect: A knot is tied in a rope and then suddenly disappears!

Secret: For this trick you will need a length of soft rope. Before performing this trick, tie a small piece of thread around the rope so that a loop is formed in the middle of the rope, as the picture shows. During your show, cover the thread with your fingers. Take one end of the rope and thread it through the loop as if you were tying a knot. If you now pull both ends of the rope apart, the thread will break and the knot in the centre will vanish!

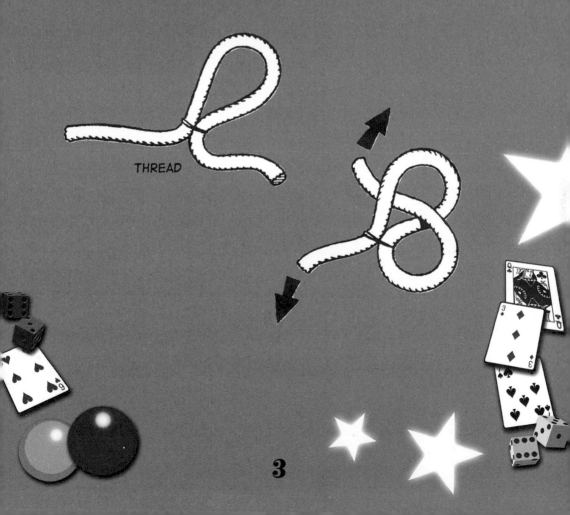

THREAD

ROPE THROUGH BODY

Effect: A rope passes through your assistant's body.

Secret: For this trick you will need a length of soft rope. Two spectators are invited to examine the rope. Put the middle of the rope against your assistant's chest and take both ends around the back of his body where you pretend to cross them over. In fact, your assistant secretly sticks up his thumbs and you wrap the rope around them as shown. Hand the ends of the rope to the spectators on either side. When you clap your hands, your assistant lowers his thumbs and walks away - free of the rope!

JUMPING KNOT

Effect: A knot tied in a length of rope leaps into the air at your command!

Secret: For this trick you will need a length of soft rope. Before you start the trick, ask an adult to cut off a small length from the end of your magic rope. Tie a loose knot in this small piece and loop the middle of the longer rope through it, as the picture shows. Now when you pull the ends of the rope quite hard, the knot will jump off the rope and into the air.

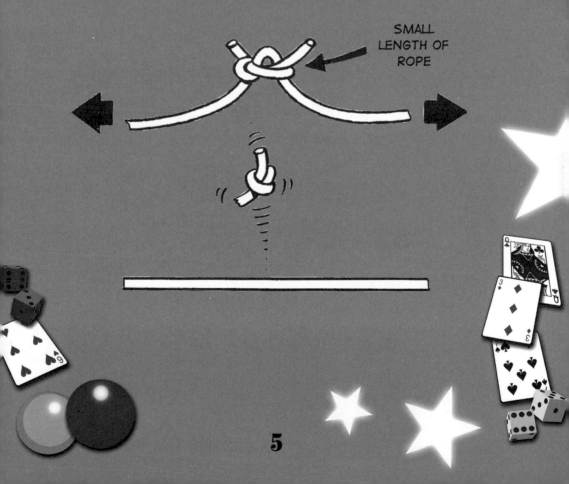

SMALL
LENGTH OF
ROPE

SELF-TYING KNOT

Effect: You can tie a knot in a rope without letting go of either end.

Secret: For this trick you will need a length of soft rope. Ask a spectator to hold on to one end of your rope with each hand and to try to tie a knot in it without letting go. After a few tries he will say it is impossible. When it is your turn, just fold your arms and keep them folded while you pick up the rope ends. Hold onto them while you unfold your arms and a knot will form in the middle of the rope!

THE FLOATING SAUSAGE

Effect: You can conjure up a sausage floating between your fingers.

Secret: This is a very funny optical illusion. Hold your two forefingers a short distance in front of your face, as the picture shows. If you relax your eyes you will see the optical illusion. A floating sausage!

THE FLOATING ARM

Effect: A spectator's arm rises mysteriously into the air at your command!

Secret: Ask a spectator to stand with his side against a wall. Explain that you are going to influence his arm, but first you will need to test his strength. Ask him to hold his arm down by his side and to push his wrist against the wall as hard as he can for about a minute. When he has done this, have him relax his arm and step away from the wall while you perform the magic. Make a magical gesture over the arm and it will start to rise up.

PUSH!

THE REMOVABLE THUMB

Effect: You appear to remove your thumb.

Secret: Try this out in front of a mirror. Hold out your left hand with the palm facing you. Bend your left thumb towards your body. Now bend your right thumb in half and place it alongside your left, as the first picture shows. Place your right forefinger over the front of the two thumbs where they touch, as in the second picture. Move your right hand to the right and it looks as if you have removed your thumb. This trick should be done only for people who are directly facing you.

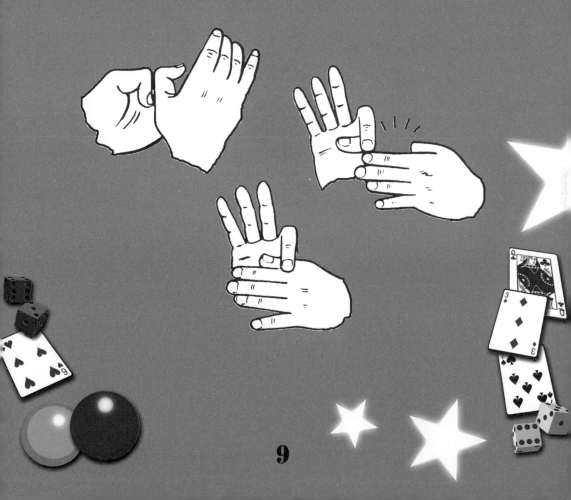

FRUIT TRANSFORMATION

Effect: An orange turns into an apple.

Secret: For this trick you will need an apple and an orange. Ask an adult to cut the peel from an orange, as the picture shows, and to scoop out all the fruit. When the peel has dried, put an apple inside it. Hold the peel closed and it looks just like an ordinary orange. To perform, cover the peel with a hanky. When you remove the hanky, take the orange peel off with it, keeping it hidden inside. Drop the hanky into your pocket or behind something on the table, as you show the apple to your audience.

REMOVE ORANGE PEEL
WITH HANDKERCHIEF

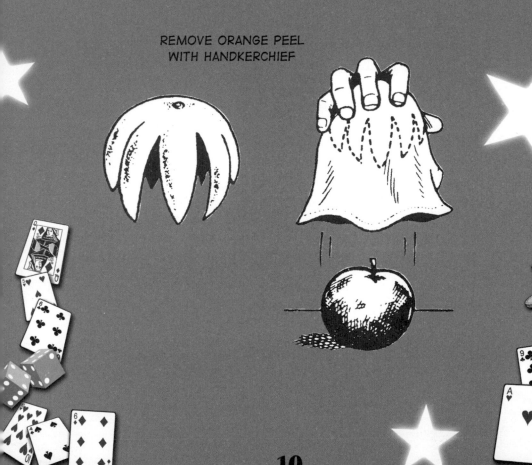

BAFFLING BANDS

Effect: Three loops of paper are cut, with surprising results!

Secret: You need three long strips of paper. Stick the ends of the first strip together to form a loop. Do the same with the second strip, but put a half-twist in it before you stick it down. The third strip is twisted completely round before sticking it. Look at the pictures to get the idea. Ask an adult to cut the loops in half, right along their lengths. The first loop will become two separate loops, as you would expect. The second loop will become a much larger loop and the third will form two linked rings!

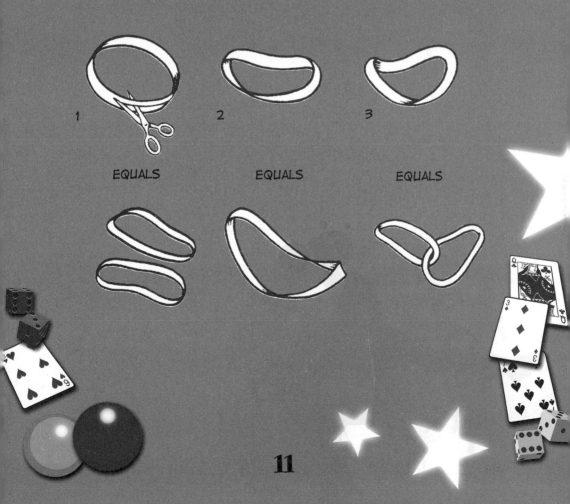

WALKING THROUGH A POSTCARD

Effect: A postcard is cut so it will go over your body.

Secret: For this trick you will require a postcard. Boast that you can walk through a postcard then make the following moves. Fold the postcard in half lengthways. Make as many cuts as possible (or ask an adult to do so) from the edge of the card to the centre and from the centre toward the edges as shown. The more cuts you make, the easier the trick is to do. Unfold the card and cut along the centre from A to B as shown. You can now open out the card into a large loop that will easily go over your body!

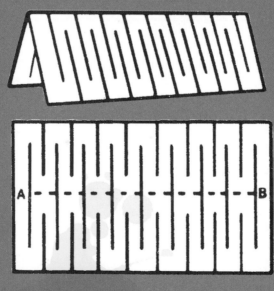

PERPLEXING PENCIL

Effect: A pencil adheres to one hand and then to the other.

Secret: The secret is a small pin pushed into the pencil. Hold the pin between the fingers of your right hand. The pencil seems to stick to the fingers. Bring your left hand to the pencil. Turn to the left and revolve the pencil between your hands. This causes the pin to move from your right fingers to your left fingers. Remove your right hand and the pencil is now apparently stuck to the left fingers. By reversing this movement, you can move the pencil back to the right hand.

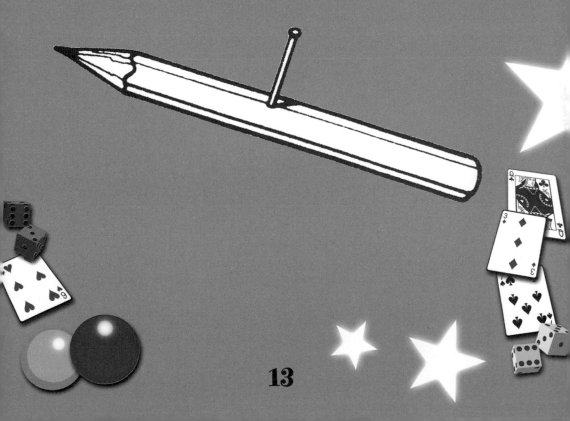

SWEETS TO THE SWEET

Effect: Sweets, appear from a handkerchief and vanish in a box!

Secret: For this trick you will need a handkerchief, some thread, a box and some sweets. Tie a wrapped sweet to a long length of thread. Sew the other end of the thread to the middle of one end of the handkerchief. Fold the handkerchief in half, hold two corners in one hand and two in the other. Tip the hanky and the sweet falls out into a box on your table. Allow the handkerchief to fall open, with the sweet hidden at the rear. Lift the hanky and repeat the above movements until you have produced enough sweets, then tip the box to show they have vanished!

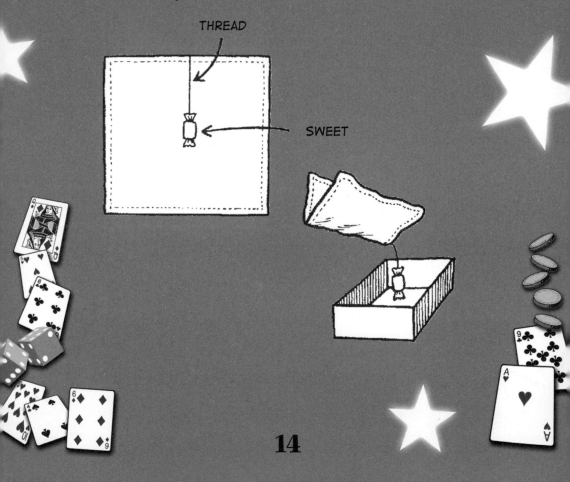

THREAD

SWEET

CHAIN REACTION

Effect: Paper clips form themselves into a chain.

Secret: Link 10 paper clips and put them in one corner of an envelope. Put a strip of glue on the inside of the envelope, just above the chain. Put 10 loose paper clips into the envelope and you are ready to show the trick. Tip out the loose clips, then drop them, one at a time, back into the envelope and seal it down. Tear off the corner of the envelope. The chain will drop out. Casually put the envelope in your pocket and display the chain of clips.

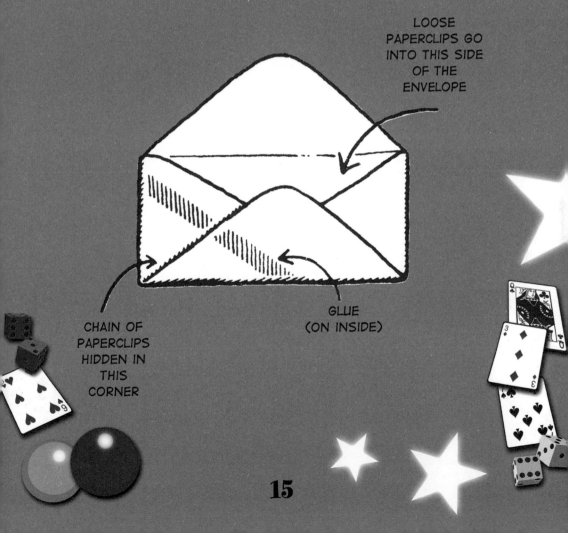

LOOSE
PAPERCLIPS GO
INTO THIS SIDE
OF THE
ENVELOPE

CHAIN OF
PAPERCLIPS
HIDDEN IN
THIS
CORNER

GLUE
(ON INSIDE)

SALT CELLAR SUSPENSION

Effect: A salt cellar is suspended from your fingertip.

Secret: All you need, apart from the salt cellar, is a toothpick. Keep the toothpick hidden behind your forefinger as you touch the salt cellar. Secretly push the toothpick into the top of the salt cellar. Hold the hidden toothpick between your thumb and forefinger and you can lift the cellar. It appears that the cellar is sticking to your finger. Take the cellar in your left hand and pull it away from the toothpick. As you hand the cellar to someone for examination, secretly drop the toothpick on to your lap.

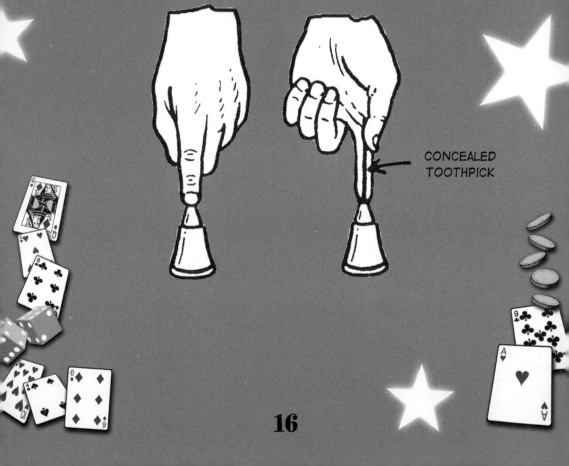

CONCEALED
TOOTHPICK

QUICK TIE HANDKERCHIEFS

Effect: Two handkerchiefs are thrown into the air where they knot themselves together.

Secret: Apart from the two handkerchiefs, all you need for this trick is a small elastic band hidden in your right hand. Pick up one of the handkerchiefs with your left hand and place it in the right. As you do so, push a corner of the handkerchief into the elastic band. Do exactly the same with the second handkerchief. Throw the two handkerchiefs into the air and catch one of them as they descend. The elastic band holds the two handkerchiefs together and they appear to be knotted.

ELASTIC BAND

MAGIC STAMP ALBUM

Effect: An empty album becomes magically filled with stamps.

Secret: You need an exercise book to make this trick. Go through the book and cut a narrow strip from the edges of every other page. On every double page where the short edge is to the right, stick some stamps. The pages where the short page is on the left should be left untouched. Flick through the pages with your right hand and it will look like an ordinary exercise book. Say some magic words and flick through the book again using your left hand and the book is filled with stamps.

CUT AND RESTORED RIBBON

Effect: A ribbon is cut in two, then restored.

Secret: You need a piece of ribbon a metre long and another piece that's eight centimetres long. Sew the short piece to the middle of the long piece. Provided you keep it moving, the short piece will not be noticed. Fold the ribbon in half and pull the centre up through your fist. In fact you pull up only the short piece. Cut through the short piece and then cut away the rest of it (including the stitched bit). You have cut the ribbon in two but you can now show it completely restored!

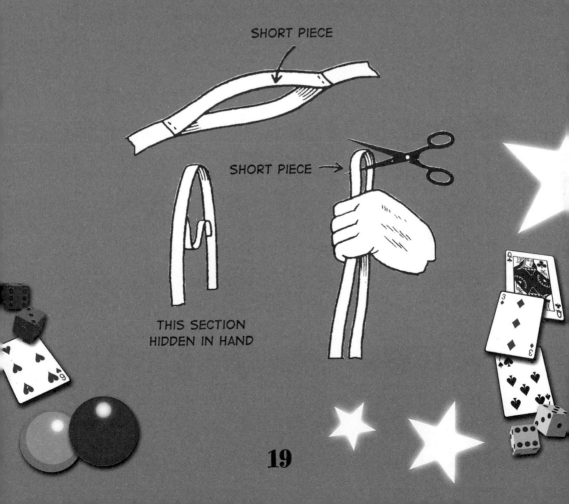

SHORT PIECE

SHORT PIECE →

THIS SECTION
HIDDEN IN HAND

UPSIDE-DOWN CUPS

Effect: No matter how they try, the spectator cannot copy what you do with the cups.

Secret: Put three cups on the table, as the first picture shows. Tell your audience that you can turn all the cups bottom-up in three moves, turning two cups over each time. *First move: turn over cups 2 and 3. Second move: turn over cups 1 and 3. Third move: turn over cups 2 and 3. All the cups are now bottom-up!* Now let a spectator try the trick, only this time set the cups up as in the second picture. No matter what they do, they will not be able to copy you!

1

1   2   3

2